The Beautiful Baking Book

igloobooks

Published in 2014
by Igloo Books Ltd
Cottage Farm
Sywell
NN6 0BJ
www.igloobooks.com

Copyright© 2014 Igloo Books Ltd

Food photography and recipe development: PhotoCuisine UK
Front and back cover images © PhotoCuisine UK

HUN001 0114
2 4 6 8 10 9 7 5 3 1
ISBN 978-1-78197-793-4

Printed and manufactured in China

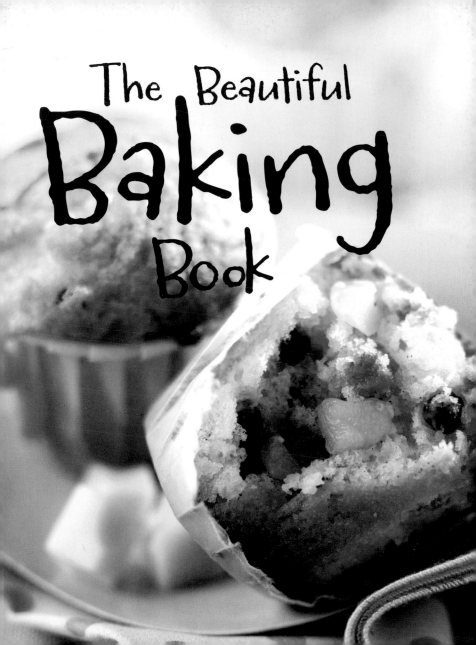

The Beautiful
Baking
Book

Contents

Strawberry Tartlet

Shortbread Cookies
with Jam Filling

Small Duck Pie

Contents

Individual Mocha Cakes

Cherry Almond Brioche Cake

Chocolate and Raspberry Fondants

Introduction

Discover how much fun you can have in the kitchen with this wonderful cookbook, filled with delicious recipes to get you baking!

Choose from any of these sweet and savoury recipes and follow the instructions to create tasty treats for any occasion. Whether you're having a party and want some fun finger food, or you want to bake stunning cakes and sweet snacks, there are loads of fantastic recipes just for you. Bake yummy pies for dinner, scrumptious chocolate brownies and much more in this small cookbook — perfect for every little chef!

With easy-to-follow instructions, this cookbook is designed specifically for kids, with helpful hints and tips and mouth-watering food photography to get your taste buds tingling! Don't forget to read the golden rules before you start, and always ask an adult for help. You'll be a great baker in no time!

Onion and Bacon Cupcakes

Pepper and Feta Pizzas

Golden Rules

Before:

1. Always ask an adult's permission before you start baking, or ask them to help you.

2. Wash your hands before you start cooking, and after too.

3. To keep your clothes clean, wear an apron.

4. Read through the recipe and check you have all of the ingredients and equipment required.

5. Measure your ingredients carefully.

During:

1. Follow the step-by-step instructions, making sure you ask an adult for help if you don't understand something.

2. Wash fruit to remove any dirt and chemicals.

3. Take extra care with scissors or knives; ask an adult to teach you or to help.

4. Always make sure you stay in the kitchen while you're cooking, and keep an eye on your dish.

5. Always use oven gloves and be careful when using the oven.

After:

1. Remember to turn the oven off when you have finished.

2. Help clean the kitchen, tidy away the equipment and wash the dishes.

3. Enjoy eating your delicious creations.

Techniques

Some of the recipes in this cookbook may contain words that you haven't used before. If you are stuck, use this list of terms and techniques to help you along, and don't forget to ask an adult for help!

Beat – Mix the ingredients in a fast up-and-down motion until they are completely mixed.

Blend – Mix the ingredients together until they are no longer separate.

Combine –Stir the ingredients together until they are completely mixed in, like blending.

Drain – Separate liquids from solids, using a colander or drainer.

Fold – Gently stir the ingredients with a spoon as though folding the ingredients into each other, to keep the air in the mixture.

Grease – Coat a tin, pan or tray with a thin layer of cooking oil or softened butter, to stop the mixture from sticking when it goes in the oven.

Incorporate – Stir in the ingredients until they are completely mixed in, like combining.

Knead – Fold the dough into itself and press it with your hands until soft and smooth.

Line – Put greaseproof or non-stick baking paper into the base and sides of a tin or tray, to stop the mixture sticking when in the oven.

Pipe – Use a piping bag, or plastic bag with a corner cut out, to decorate food with a topping. This is called piping.

Sift – Remove lumps from dry ingredients by pressing or shaking through a sieve or mesh strainer.

Simmer – Cook the liquid on a low heat so that the mixture does not boil, but small bubbles form on the surface.

Stiff Peaks – Whisk egg whites until the mixture is thick enough to stand up by itself. Use the whisk to pull the mixture upward, it should form a 'stiff peak'.

Strain – Use a colander or strainer to drain liquids from cooking foods, like draining.

Whip – Beat your ingredients together quickly with a spoon until the mixture is light and fluffy.

Whisk – Mix ingredients together in a side-to-side motion using a whisk, to get air into the mixture.

Useful Utensils

Before you start cooking, make sure you know exactly what equipment you will need for the recipe, and have it all prepared before you start cooking. Always ask an adult to help you with equipment that you haven't used before! Here is a list of useful utensils that you may need to bake these yummy treats:

Baking Tins	Pastry Brush
Baking Tray	Piping Bag
Chopping Board	Ramekins
Cupcake Tray	Rolling Pin
Electric Whisk	Saucepans with Lids
Greaseproof Paper	Scissors
Heatproof Bowl	Shaped Cutters
Individual Tartlet Cases	Sieve
Knives	Skewer
Lemon Squeezer	Spoons for Measuring
Mixing Bowls	Teaspoon
Moulds	Weighing Scales
Oven Gloves	Whisk
Ovenproofed Trays and Dishes	Wire Rack
Palette Knife	Wooden or Metal Spoon

Sweet

Stained Glass
Lollipop Biscuits

Cream Tea Scones

Pink Iced Cookies

Summer Fruit Linzertorte

Medium   Preparation time: 15–20 minutes   Serves: 8   Cooking time: 20–25 minutes

Ingredients

- 350 g / 12 oz / 3 cups raspberries
- 200 g / 7 oz / 2 cups cranberries
- 110 g / 4 oz / ½ cup caster (superfine) sugar
- 2 tbsp cold water
- 1 tbsp arrowroot (mixed with 1 tbsp of cold water)
- 350 g / 9 oz ready-made shortcrust pastry
- a little plain (all purpose) flour, for dusting
- 1 large egg, beaten

TOP TIP

This torte goes really well with vanilla ice cream or a drizzle of cream.

Method

1. With the help of an adult, preheat the oven to 180°C (160°C fan) / 350F / gas 4 and place the fruit, sugar and 2 tbsp of cold water in a saucepan; cook for 5 minutes until syrupy, then stir in the arrowroot mixture.

2. Roll out the pastry on a floured surface to ½ cm thickness and use it to line an 8" x 4" x 2" fluted tart tin. Cut off the leftover pastry and re-roll to ½ cm before cutting into strips.

3. Prick the base with a fork, fill with the fruit mixture and arrange the pastry strips in a criss-cross on top; brush the pastry with egg.

4. Bake the torte for 20-25 minutes until the pastry is cooked and golden-brown.

5. Ask an adult to help remove the linzertorte and let it cool before serving.

Strawberry Tartlet

Easy

Preparation time: 20 minutes

Makes: 4

Cooking time: 15 minutes

Ingredients

- 110 g / 4 oz / ⅔ cup plain (all purpose) flour
- a little extra plain (all-purpose) flour, for dusting
- 110 g / 4 oz / ½ cup unsalted butter, cold and cubed
- 2-3 tbsp iced water
- 1 tbsp caster (superfine) sugar
- 600 g / 1 lb 5 oz / 3 cups ready made custard, chilled

To Garnish

- 30 g / 1 oz / ½ cup icing (confectioners') sugar
- 8 large strawberries
- ½ lemon, juiced
- a canister of extra-thick spray cream

TOP TIP

Get creative by shaking some sprinkles on top of the cream.

Method

1. With the supervision of an adult, cut the strawberries in half using a sharp knife.

2. Place them in a bowl and sprinkle over the icing sugar and lemon juice, stirring well until the icing sugar has all disappeared.

3. Place the flour, sugar and butter in a bowl, rubbing the butter into the flour and sugar with fingertips until the mixture resembles breadcrumbs.

4. Add the water, one tablespoon at a time, and mix until a soft dough starts to come together. Knead on a surface a few times, shape into a ball and wrap in cling film before chilling for 30 minutes.

5. Roll the pastry out on a floured surface to ½ cm thickness and cut out four rounds to line individual tartlet cases.

6. Prick with a fork, line with greaseproof paper and baking beans and bake for 15 minutes. Remove to a wire rack, with an adult's help, and discard the paper and beans. Allow to cool.

7. Spoon the custard into the pastry and then place four strawberry halves on top of the custard.

8. You can chill the tartlets at this point if you want to eat them later; if not, squirt some cream on top of each before eating.

Small Raspberry Meringues

Medium   Preparation time: 15–20 minutes   Serves: 8   Cooking time: 60 minutes

Ingredients

- 2 large egg whites
- a pinch of salt
- 110 g / 4 oz / ½ cup caster (superfine) sugar
- 1 tsp raspberry flavouring
- a few drops of natural red food dye

TOP TIP
These meringues are really yummy with a dollop of whipped cream and some fresh raspberries.

Method

1. Ask an adult to help you preheat the oven to 130°C (110°C fan) / 250F / gas ½ and line two large baking trays with greaseproof paper.

2. Whisk the egg whites in a large, clean bowl with a pinch of salt until they start to form soft peaks.

3. Add half the sugar, the raspberry flavouring and some red food dye, and keep beating until it starts to turn stiff.

4. Add the remaining sugar and keep beating for another 3-4 minutes. Ask an adult to help you out and give your arm a rest!

5. Spoon the mixture into a piping bag fitted with a star-shaped nozzle, pipe blobs onto the trays, and bake for one hour until set.

6. Turn the oven off with the help of an adult and let the meringues cool before enjoying.

Shortbread Cookies with Jam Filling

Medium   Preparation time: 10-15 minutes   Makes: 8   Cooking time: 12-15 minutes

Ingredients

- 300 g / 10 ½ oz / 2 cups plain (all purpose) flour
- a little extra plain (all-purpose) flour, for dusting
- 225 g / 8 oz / 1 cup unsalted butter, melted and cooled
- 65 g / 2 ½ oz / ½ cup icing (confectioners') sugar
- 50 g / 2 oz / ⅓ cup cornflour (cornstarch)
- a pinch of salt

For the filling

- 300 g / 10 ½ oz / 1 ⅓ cups strawberry jam (jelly), warmed

Method

1. Mix the cookie ingredients in a mixing bowl until they come together as a dough. Knead it briefly before wrapping and chilling for 60 minutes.

2. Ask an adult to help preheat the oven to 180°C (160°C fan) / 350F / gas 4 and line two baking trays with greaseproof paper.

3. Roll out the dough on a floured surface to ½ cm thickness and cut out 16 circles using a fluted, round cookie cutter and arrange on the trays.

4. Use a small star-shaped cutter to punch stars from half of the circles. Bake for 12-15 minutes until golden before asking an adult to move them to a wire rack.

5. Once cool, spread the half without holes with jam before sandwiching with the remaining star-cut half.

TOP TIP

Bake the star cuttings with the cookies for an additional treat and dust the finished stars with a little icing sugar for a sweet taste.

Individual Redcurrent Cheesecakes

Easy   Preparation time: 10 minutes   Makes: 6   Cooking time: 10 minutes

Ingredients

- 175 g / 6 oz / 1 ½ cups pink wafer biscuits, crushed
- 50 g / 2 oz / ½ cup butter, melted and cooled
- 30 ml / 1 fl. oz / 2 tbsp lemon juice
- 2 sheets gelatine
- 225 g / 8 oz / 1 cup low-fat cream cheese
- 110 g / 4 oz / ½ cup caster (superfine) sugar
- 225 g / 8 oz / 1 cup Greek yoghurt
- 175 g / 6 oz / 1 ½ cups redcurrants, washed

To garnish

- 36 small sprigs of redcurrants

TOP TIP

You could try swapping the redcurrants on top for a teaspoon of warm redcurrant jelly.

Method

1 Stir together crushed wafers with the butter in a mixing bowl and then pack into the base of six individual cheesecake moulds; chill until needed.

2. Mix the lemon juice and gelatine in a saucepan and dissolve over a medium heat, stirring occasionally.

3. Beat together the cream cheese and the sugar in a large mixing bowl, and then add the Greek yoghurt and the gelatine mixture, mixing again until smooth.

4. Crush the redcurrants before folding through the cheesecake mixture and spooning into the moulds. Chill the mixture for at least 3 hours.

5. Once set, ask an adult to run a warm knife around the edge of the cheesecakes to help them release, then place onto serving plates.

6. Garnish with sprigs of redcurrants on top.

Cream Tea Scones

Medium   Preparation time: 10-15 minutes   Makes: 6   Cooking time: 15-20 minutes

Ingredients

- 55 g / 2 oz / ½ cup butter, cold and cubed
- 225 g / 8 oz / 1 ½ cups self-raising flour
- a pinch of salt
- 30 g / 1 oz / 2 tbsp caster (superfine) sugar
- 150 ml / 5 fl. oz / ⅔ cup semi-skimmed milk
- a little plain (all purpose) flour, for dusting
- 1 small egg, beaten

To serve

- 225 g / 8 oz / 1 cup extra-thick cream whipped
- 175 g / 6 oz / ½ cup strawberry jam (jelly)

Method

1. With an adult's help, preheat the oven to 200°C (180°C fan) / 400F / gas 6 and line a large baking tray with greaseproof paper.

2. Rub the butter into the flour and salt in a mixing bowl, and then stir in the sugar and the milk to form a soft dough.

3. Turn it onto a floured surface, pat into a round, and roll out to 2 cm thick. Use a 3-4" cutter to stamp out six rounds before arranging them on the tray.

4. Brush the tops with beaten egg and bake for 15-20 minutes until golden and risen.

5. Ask an adult to help remove them from the oven and place on a wire rack to cool.

6. When they are cool, split in half and serve with lots of cream and jam.

TOP TIP

Change things up by using blackcurrant jam instead of the traditional strawberry.

Stained Glass Lollipop Biscuits

Medium   Preparation time: 10-15 minutes   Makes: 24   Cooking time: 15-18 minutes

Ingredients

- 300 g / 10 ½ oz / 2 cups plain (all purpose) flour
- 225 g / 8 oz / 1 cup unsalted butter, softened
- 175 g / 6 oz / ½ cup caster (superfine) sugar
- 2 small egg yolks
- 1 tsp vanilla extract
- a pinch of salt
- 24 assorted boiled sweets (hard candies)
- 24 lollipop sticks, soaked in cold water for 30 minutes beforehand

Method

1. Mix together the butter, sugar, vanilla and salt until smooth before adding the egg yolks and beating well.

2. Stir in the flour until you have an even dough and roll into a 5 cm log; ask an adult to help you with this.

3. Wrap and chill it for 60 minutes before asking an adult to preheat the oven to 180°C (160° fan) / 350F / gas 4 and line two baking trays with greaseproof paper.

4. Cut the dough into ½ cm thick rounds and, with the help of an adult, cut out shapes in the dough.

5. Arrange the dough on trays and place a boiled sweet in their holes before inserting the sticks; bake for 15-18 minutes until the sweets have melted and spread.

6. Let the cookies cool completely before serving.

TOP TIP

Substitute 50 g of the flour for the same amount of cocoa powder for a chocolatey twist.

Nut Crunch Brownies

Medium · Preparation time: 10 minutes · Serves: 8–10 · Cooking time: 35–40 minutes

Ingredients

- 350 g / 12 oz / 2 cups good-quality dark chocolate, chopped
- 225 g / 8 oz / 1 cup unsalted butter, softened
- 3 large eggs
- 250 g / 9 oz / 1 ⅓ cups light soft brown sugar
- 110 g / 4 oz / ⅔ cup plain (all-purpose) flour
- 1 tsp baking powder
- 175 g / 6 oz / 1 ½ cups pecans, chopped
- 110 g / 4 oz / 1 cup Brazil nuts, chopped
- a pinch of salt

Method

1. Preheat the oven, with an adult's help, to 170°C (150°C fan) / 325°F / gas 3 and grease and line a 6" square tin with greaseproof paper.

2. Melt the chocolate and butter in a saucepan, stirring occasionally until smooth before setting to one side.

3. Whisk the eggs in a bowl until thick, then add the sugar and continue to whisk until glossy before beating in the melted chocolate mixture.

4. Fold in the flour, baking powder and half of the pecans before pouring into the pan; sprinkle the remaining nuts on top.

5. Bake for 35-40 minutes until the surface has set; test with a wooden toothpick, if it comes out almost clean, it's done.

6. Ask an adult to remove the brownie from the oven. Let it cool before turning out and enjoying.

TOP TIP

If you don't like nuts, you can swap them for fresh raspberries, stirring them into the mixture.

Pink Iced Cookies

Medium

Preparation time: 15 minutes

Makes: 24

Cooking time: 18–22 minutes

Ingredients

- 225 g / 8 oz / 1 cup unsalted butter, softened
- 175 g / 6 oz / ½ cup caster (superfine) sugar
- 1 ½ tsp vanilla extract
- a pinch of salt
- 2 medium egg yolks
- 300 g / 10 ½ oz / 2 cups plain (all purpose) flour
- 250 g / 9 oz ready-made pink fondant icing
- a little icing (confectioners') sugar, for dusting
- 75 g / 3 oz / ⅓ cup apricot jam (jelly), warmed
- 75 g / 3 oz / ½ cup silver dragee balls

Method

1. Mix together the butter, sugar, vanilla and salt until smooth before adding the egg yolks and mixing well.

2. Stir in the flour until you have an even dough and roll into a log, before wrapping and chilling for 60 minutes.

3. Ask an adult to preheat the oven to 180°C (160°C fan) / 350F / gas 4 and line two baking trays with greaseproof paper.

4. With an adult watching, cut 1 cm rounds from the dough and arrange on the trays. Bake for 18-22 minutes until golden, then ask an adult to remove to a wire rack.

5. Roll out the icing on icing sugar to ½ cm before stamping out fluted rounds.

6. Dab the top of the cookies with jam and secure the icing to them, studding with dragee balls before eating.

TOP TIP

You can change the colour of the icing to anything you want — red, blue, or green

28

Star-Shaped Shortbread Cookies

Easy | Preparation time: 10-15 minutes | Makes: 24 | Cooking time: 12-15 minutes

Ingredients

- 300 g / 10 ½ oz / 2 cups plain (all purpose) flour
- 225 g / 8 oz / 1 cup unsalted butter, melted and cooled
- 65 g / 2 ½ oz / ½ cup icing (confectioners') sugar
- 50 g / 2 oz / ⅓ cup cornflour (cornstarch)
- 1 tsp vanilla extract
- a pinch of salt
- a little extra plain (all-purpose) flour, for dusting

To decorate

- 50 g / 2 oz / ½ cup caster (superfine) sugar
- 1 tbsp pink sugar crystals

Method

1. Mix the cookie ingredients in a mixing bowl until it comes together as a dough. Knead briefly before wrapping and chilling for 60 minutes.

2. Ask an adult to help preheat the oven to 180°C (160°C fan) / 350F / gas 4 and line two baking trays with greaseproof paper.

3. Roll out the dough on a floured surface to ½ cm thickness and cut out 24 stars using a star-shaped cookie cutter.

4. Arrange the stars on the trays and bake for 12-15 minutes until golden, before asking an adult to move them to a wire rack.

5. Dust the cookies with caster sugar as they cool and decorate with pink sugar crystals.

6. You can stack and wrap the cookies in bundles if you like.

TOP TIP

For a nutty alternative, replace the cornflour with ground almonds in the cookie dough.

Sweet Muffins

Easy   Preparation time: 10 minutes   Makes: 16   Cooking time: 20-25 minutes

Ingredients

- 150 g / 5 oz / ⅔ cup golden caster (superfine) sugar
- 300 g / 10 ½ oz / 2 cups plain (all purpose) flour
- ½ tsp salt
- 3 tsp baking powder
- 100 g / 3 ½ oz / ⅔ cup milk chocolate chips
- 1 large egg
- 110 ml / 4 fl. oz / ½ cup sunflower oil
- 225 ml / 8 fl. oz / 1 cup whole milk
- 50 g / 2 oz / ⅓ cup cocoa powder

Method

1. Preheat the oven with an adult's help to 190°C (170°C fan) / 375F / gas 5 and line a large muffin tin with 16 cases.

2. Mix the sugar, flour, salt, baking powder and chocolate chips in a bowl; add the egg, oil and three-quarters of the milk and stir briefly until you have a lumpy yet moist batter.

3. Divide the mixture between two bowls and add the cocoa and remaining milk to one bowl, stirring gently to incorporate the cocoa.

4. Spoon the separate batters into cases and bake for 20-25 minutes until risen and a cake tester comes out clean from their centres.

5. Ask an adult to move the muffin tray to a wire rack to cool. These muffins are best eaten slightly warm.

TOP TIP

Adding a handful of raisins to the muffin batters adds a chewy texture.

Lemon Meringue Tartlet

 Medium

 Preparation time: 15 minutes

 Serves: 4

 Cooking time: 12–15 minutes

Ingredients

- 1 medium egg white
- a pinch of salt
- 55 g / 2 oz / ¼ cup caster (superfine) sugar
- ½ tsp cream of tartar
- 4 x ready-made tartlet cases
- 450 g / 1 lb / 2 cups lemon curd

To garnish

- 4 cocktail cherries

Method

1. Ask an adult to preheat the oven to 220°C (200°C fan) / 425F / gas 7 and line a baking tray with greaseproof paper.

2. Whisk the egg white in a bowl with a pinch of salt until you get soft peaks.

3. Add the sugar and cream of tartar and keep whisking until glossy and really thick. Spoon the mixture into a piping bag that's been fitted with a star-shaped nozzle.

4. Pipe rounds of the meringue onto the baking tray, leaving small holes in the centre of the rounds before baking for 12-15 minutes until set and coloured on top; ask an adult to move the tray to a wire rack.

5. Fill the pastry cases with lemon curd and sit the meringue on top, garnish it with a cherry before eating.

TOP TIP

For a different citrus twist, try using lime or orange curd instead of lemon.

Apple Tartlets

Medium | Preparation time: 10-15 minutes | Makes: 6 | Cooking time: 15-18 minutes

Ingredients

- 200 g / 7 oz ready-made puff pastry
- a little plain (all purpose) flour, for dusting
- 2 Granny Smith apples, peeled, cored and halved
- 30 g / 1 oz / 2 tbsp caster (superfine) sugar
- 55 g / 2 oz / ½ cup unsalted butter, cut into small cubes

TOP TIP

You could easily use nectarine slices instead of apple for a different flavour and colour.

Method

1. Ask an adult to help you preheat the oven to 200°C (180°C fan) / 400F / gas 6, and line a large baking tray with greaseproof paper.

2. Dust a surface with flour and roll out the pastry to 12" x 6" x ½". Ask an adult to help you with the size.

3. Cut evenly into six and arrange on the tray, pricking them with a fork.

4. Get an adult to help you cut the apples thinly and arrange them on the pastry, so that they overlap. Make sure to leave a border.

5. Sprinkle the tops with sugar and dot with little cubes of butter. Bake for 15-18 minutes until puffed and golden at the edges.

6. Get an adult to help you remove them to a wire rack to cool before enjoying.

36

Ice Cream Cone Cookies

Difficult

Preparation time: 10 minutes

Makes: 24

Cooking time: 15-18 minutes

Ingredients

- 150 g / 5 oz / ⅔ cup butter, melted
- 100 g / 3 ½ oz / ½ cup golden caster (superfine) sugar
- 175 g / 6 oz / 1 cup soft light brown sugar
- 1 tsp vanilla extract
- 1 medium egg
- 1 medium egg yolk
- 250 g / 9 oz / 1 ⅔ cups plain (all purpose) flour
- ½ tsp salt
- ½ tsp bicarbonate of (baking) soda

To decorate

- 125 g / 4 ½ oz / ½ cup pink fondant icing
- 125 g / 4 ½ oz / ½ cup light blue fondant icing
- white and pink icing pens
- 150 g / 5 oz / 1 cup milk chocolate, melted
- 24 red jelly beans

Method

1. Preheat the oven, with an adult's help, to 180°C (160°C fan) / 350F / gas 4 and line two baking trays.

2. Mix together the butter and sugars thoroughly in a bowl, then add the vanilla, egg and egg yolk. Mix again then stir in the flour, salt and bicarbonate of soda to make a dough.

3. Drop the dough onto the trays and roughly shape into ice cream cone shapes before baking for 15-18 minutes until dark golden. Ask an adult to remove them.

4. Roll the icings out thinly and cut out scoop shapes before attaching them to the cookies with icing from the pens.

5. Make criss-cross patterns on the cookies with melted chocolate and let it set. Then, make an outline on the icing with the pens and secure the beans to them.

TOP TIP

Add chocolate chips to the cookie dough for an extra chocolatey flavour in these cookies.

Assorted Macaroons

Difficult   Preparation time: 15 minutes   Makes: 24   Cooking time: 8–10 minutes

Ingredients

- 300 g / 10 ½ oz / 3 cups ground almonds
- 450 g / 1lb / 3 ½ cups icing (confectioners') sugar, sifted
- 4 medium egg whites
- a pinch of salt
- 1 tsp natural red food dye
- ½ tsp natural green food dye
- ½ tsp of orange food dye
- 30 g / 1 oz / 2 tbsp cocoa powder

For the fillings

- 250 g / 9 oz / 1 cup ready-made buttercream icing
- 100 g / 3 ½ oz / ⅔ cup chocolate spread
- 75 g / 3 oz / ⅓ cup strawberry jam (jelly)
- 75 g / 3 oz / ⅓ cup passion fruit puree
- 55 g / 2 oz / ½ cup unsalted pistachios, shelled and finely chopped

Method

1. Ask an adult to preheat the oven to 180°C (160°C fan) / 350F / gas 4 and line baking trays.

2. Mix the ground almonds and icing sugar in one bowl. Beat the egg whites in another bowl with a pinch of salt until stiff, then fold the whites into the almonds.

3. Divide between four bowls and colour three of them. Fold the cocoa powder into the fourth.

4. Spoon into separate piping bags fitted with nozzles and pipe rounds onto the trays before leaving for 15 minutes and then baking for 8-10 minutes.

5. Ask an adult to move the trays to wire racks to cool. Mix a quarter of the buttercream with the pistachios, a quarter with strawberry jam, a quarter with passion fruit puree and quarter with chocolate spread.

6. Spread and sandwich the fillings on corresponding macaroons. Strawberry jam for red, chocolate spread for chocolate, passion fruit puree for orange and pistachio for green.

TOP TIP

Fold a small handful of chopped almonds into the macaroon mixture for a crunchier texture.

Savoury

Ham and
Cheese Cupcakes

Small Duck Pie

Pepper and Feta Pizza

Goats' Cheese Turnovers

Medium   Preparation time: 15–20 minutes   Makes: 12   Cooking time: 15–20 minutes

Ingredients

- 30 g / 1 oz / 2 tbsp unsalted butter
- 4 medium onions, finely sliced
- 1 tsp caster (superfine) sugar
- salt and pepper
- 350 g / 12 oz ready-made puff pastry
- a little plain (all-purpose) flour, for dusting
- 150 g / 5 oz / 1 cup goats' cheese, cubed
- 1 large egg, beaten

Method

1. Ask an adult to help preheat the ove
   to 190°C (170°C fan) / 375F / gas 5

2. Melt the butter in a frying pan over
   a medium heat and fry the onions
   with the sugar, salt and pepper befor
   reducing the heat and cooking them
   until they are brown.

3. Roll out the pastry on a floured
   surface to ½ cm thickness and cut ou
   12 rounds, about 10 cm across.

4. Spoon the onion onto them and dot
   with goats' cheese before folding one
   end over the other and sealing with
   fork. Ask an adult for guidance.

5. Place on a tray and brush with egg
   before baking for 15-20 minutes unt
   puffed and golden.

6. Ask an adult to help you remove the
   hot turnovers from the oven and lea
   them to cool before eating.

TOP TIP

For some colour, substitute
one of the onions for a
sliced red pepper.

Small Duck Pie

Medium   Preparation time: 20 minutes   Serves: 4   Cooking time: 15-20 minutes

Ingredients

- 30 ml / 1 fl. oz / 2 tbsp sunflower oil
- 2 medium carrot, peeled and chopped
- 1 stick of celery, finely chopped
- 1 large onion, finely chopped
- 1 clove of garlic, finely chopped
- 2 cooked duck legs, meat shredded
- 2 tsp Worcestershire sauce
- salt and pepper
- 150 g / 5 oz ready-made puff pastry
- a little plain (all-purpose) flour, for dusting
- 1 large egg, beaten

Method

1. Ask an adult to help you preheat the oven to 190°C (170°C fan) / 375F / gas 5.

2. Heat the oil in a saucepan set over a medium heat and sweat the vegetables and garlic for 8-10 minutes, stirring occasionally, until softened and starting to brown.

3. Stir through the duck, Worcestershire sauce and seasoning before spooning into four individual ramekins.

4. Roll out the pastry on a floured surface to 1 cm thickness, before cutting four rounds and carefully draping them over the duck and sealing them to the rims with a fork.

5. Brush the top with egg and make a hole in the middle before baking for 15-20 minutes, until the pastry is golden and puffed.

6. Get an adult to carefully remove the hot pies from the oven and let them cool before eating.

TOP TIP

You can change the duck for cooked beef mince if you'd like.

Tomato and Courgette Tartlet

Medium   Preparation time: 10 minutes   Serves: 6   Cooking time: 18-22 minutes

Ingredients

- 125 g / 4 ½ oz ready-made puff pastry
- a little plain (all purpose) flour, for dusting
- 30 ml / 1 fl. oz / 2 tbsp extra-virgin olive oil
- 1 courgette (zucchini), peeled and thinly sliced
- 250 g / 9 oz / 2 ½ cups vine cherry tomatoes, halved
- 75 g / 3 ½ oz / ½ cup goats' cheese
- a handful of tarragon leaves, finely chopped
- 75 g / 3 ½ oz / ½ cup pine nuts
- a small handful of picked basil leaves

TOP TIP

Swapping the goats' cheese for tangy blue cheese provides an alternative, if you're adventurous!

Method

1. Ask an adult to help you preheat the oven to 190°C (170°C fan) / 375F / gas 5.

2. Roll out the pastry on a floured surface into an 8" round before lifting it onto a baking tray and drizzling with olive oil.

3. Layer slices of courgette on top, keeping about 2 cm around the edge for the crust.

4. Arrange the halved tomatoes on top, crumble over the goats' cheese and scatter the chopped tarragon and pine nuts across the courgettes.

5. Bake for 18-22 minutes until the border is puffed and golden and the base is cooked through.

6. Ask an adult to help you remove the tartlet from the oven; let it cool a little before slicing and garnishing with basil leaves.

Sun-dried Tomato Muffins

Easy   Preparation time: 10 minutes   Makes: 12   Cooking time: 18–22 minutes

Ingredients

- 4 medium eggs
- 350 g / 12 oz / 2 ⅔ cups plain (all-purpose) flour, sifted
- 2 tsp baking powder
- 30 ml / 1 fl. oz / 2 tbsp sunflower oil
- 30 g / 1 oz / 2 tbsp butter, melted
- salt and pepper
- 110 g / 4 oz / 1 cup Cheddar, grated
- 55 g / 2 oz / ½ cup Parmesan, finely grated
- 110 g / 4 oz / ⅔ cup preserved sun-dried tomatoes, drained and chopped

Method

1. Ask an adult to help you preheat the oven to 180°C (160°C fan) / 350F / gas 4 and line a 12-hole muffin tin with paper cases.

2. Beat the eggs with a whisk in a large bowl until frothy before adding the flour, baking powder, sunflower oil, butter and some seasoning. Whisk well.

3. Stir in most of both cheeses and all the sun-dried tomato until just mixed, then spoon the batter into the cases and sprinkle the rest of the cheeses on top of the batter.

4. Bake for 18-22 minutes until a cake tester comes out clean from their centres. Ask an adult to move the hot muffin tin to a wire rack to cool.

5. Once cool, remove the muffins from their cases before enjoying!

TOP TIP
You can add 1 tsp dried rosemary to the batter for a herby twist.

Pepper and Feta Pizzas

Medium

Preparation time: 15 minutes

Makes: 4 Individual Pizzas

Cooking time: 12–15 minutes

Ingredients

· 300 g / 10 ½ oz ready-made pizza dough, divided into four balls
· a little plain (all purpose) flour, for dusting
· 2 large red peppers, deseeded and thinly sliced
· 2 large yellow peppers, deseeded and thinly sliced
· 150 g / 5 oz / 1 ½ cups feta, cubed
· 1 tsp dried oregano
· 30 ml / 1 fl. oz / 2 tbsp olive oil
· salt and pepper

Method

1. Start by asking an adult to help you preheat the oven to 200°C (180°C fan) / 400F / gas 6.

2. Roll each ball of dough into a 12-14 cm round on a floured work surface then arrange on two large baking trays.

3. Arrange a mixture of the sliced peppers in a wheel pattern on each round of dough. Cover the feta in the oregano and place on top of the peppers.

4. Drizzle the pizzas with olive oil, sprinkle with a little seasoning and bake for 12-15 minutes until the base and crust is golden-brown and cooked.

5. Ask an adult to help you remove them from the oven and make sure to let them cool a little before eating.

TOP TIP

For a different texture, replace the red pepper with halved cherry tomatoes.

Sausage Rolls

Medium   Preparation time: 15 minutes   Makes: 32   Cooking time: 15 minutes

Ingredients

- 400 g / 14 oz ready-made puff pastry, divided into two
- a little plain (all-purpose) flour, for dusting
- 32 cocktail sausages
- 2 medium eggs, beaten
- 45 g / 1 ½ oz / ⅓ cup black poppy seeds

Method

1. Ask an adult to preheat the oven to 200°C (180°C fan) / 400F / gas 6.

2. Roll out the pastry pieces on a floured surface to approximately 50 cm x 25 cm x 1 cm.

3. Position the cocktail sausages at even intervals on one piece before wetting your fingertip and rubbing it around each sausage.

4. Place the other piece of pastry on top and carefully press down and around the sausages to seal them together. Brush with egg and sprinkle the poppy seeds on top.

5. With the help of an adult, use a knife to cut through the pastry and around the sausages before arranging them on lined baking trays.

6. Bake for 15 minutes until puffed. Ask an adult to help you move them to a wire rack to cool before eating.

TOP TIP

For a different flavour, use sesame seeds instead of poppy seeds.

Onion and Bacon Cupcakes

Difficult   Preparation time: 20 minutes   Makes: 12   Cooking time: 18–22 minutes

Ingredients

- 4 medium eggs
- 350 g / 12 oz / 2 ⅓ cups plain (all purpose) flour, sifted
- 55 g / 2 oz / ½ cup butter, melted
- 2 tsp baking powder
- 225 g / 8 oz / 2 cups Red Leicester (or equivalent), finely grated
- 1 large onion, grated
- salt and pepper

For the garnish

- 12 rashers streaky bacon
- 150 g / 5 oz / 1 cup pancetta, cut into small lardons
- 2 tbsp brown sauce
- 500 g / 1 lb 2 oz / 2 cups sour cream
- 2 little gem lettuce, leaves separated and washed

Method

1. Ask an adult to help you preheat the oven to 180°C (160°C fan) / 350°F / gas 4 and line a 12-hole cupcake tin with paper cases.

2. Beat the eggs in a mixing bowl until light and frothy then the flour, butter and baking powder and mix until smooth.

3. Fold in the cheese, onion and seasoning then spoon into cases and bake for 18-22 minutes until a cake tester comes out clean.

4. Get an adult to help you grill the bacon until cooked and fry the pancetta in a pan until golden-brown. Secure the bacon around the cupcakes.

5. Fit a piping bag with a star-shaped nozzle and fill with sour cream before piping swirls on top of the cupcakes.

6. Sit gem lettuce leaves on top, fill with lardons and drizzle with brown sauce.

TOP TIP

If you prefer, switch the brown sauce for tomato ketchup.

Mediterranean Focaccia Loaf

Medium   Preparation time: 15 minutes   Serves: 8   Cooking time: 25-30 minutes

Ingredients

- 250 g / 9 oz / 1 ⅔ cups strong white bread flour
- 1 tsp salt
- 1 tsp dried active yeast (stirred into the tepid water 15 minutes beforehand)
- 150 ml / 5 fl. oz / ⅔ cup tepid water
- 30 ml / 1 fl. oz / 2 tbsp extra-virgin olive oil
- 75 g / 3 oz / ½ cup sun-dried tomatoes, drained, dried and chopped
- 100 g / 3 ½ oz / ⅔ cup pitted black olives, chopped
- 100 g / 3 ½ oz / 1 cup grated mozzarella
- a little plain (all purpose) flour, for dusting

Method

1. Preheat the oven, with an adult's help, to 190°C (170°C fan) / 375F / gas 5 and grease and line a 2 lb loaf tin with greaseproof paper.

2. Mix the flour and salt in a large mixing bowl before adding the yeast water, olive oil, tomato olives and mozzarella. Mix until you have a rough dough.

3. Flour a work surface, tip the dough onto it and knead well, for 8-10 minutes until smooth and springy.

4. Rest the dough in a covered bowl, in a warm place for 30 minutes.

5. Knead the dough briefly before shaping into the tin and baking for 25-30 minutes until golden and risen.

6. Remove it from the oven with the help of an adult and let it cool before serving.

TOP TIP

Try adding some dried herbs, such as basil and oregano, for an added Mediterranean flavour boost.

Ham and Cheese Cupcakes

Easy   Preparation time: 40 minutes   Makes: 12   Cooking time: 20-25 minutes

Ingredients

- 150 g / 5 oz / 1 cup self-raising flour
- ½ tsp baking powder (soda)
- 150 g / 5 oz / ⅔ cup margarine, softened
- 75 g / 3 oz / ½ cup Parmesan, grated
- 3 medium eggs
- 100 g / 3 ½ oz / 1 cup frozen peas, thawed
- 75 g / 3 oz / ½ cup gammon, cubed
- 75 g / 3 oz / ½ cup Mozzarella, cubed
- salt and pepper

Method

1. Preheat the oven, with an adult's supervision, to 180°C (160°C fan) / 350F / gas 4 and line a 12-hole cupcake tin with cases.

2. Mix together the flour, baking powder, margarine, Parmesan, eggs and seasoning in a mixing bowl with a handheld whisk.

3. Tip in the peas, gammon and Mozzarella and stir well until they are mixed in.

4. Spoon into the cases and bake for 20-25 minutes until risen and a cake tester comes out clean from their centres.

5. Ask an adult to remove them from the hot oven. Let them cool on a wire rack before enjoying.

TOP TIP

Use your favourite kind of cheese in the cupcakes instead of Mozzarella.

Individual Granary Breads

Difficult   **Preparation time: 20–25 minutes + 2 hours resting time**   **Makes: 12**   **Cooking time: 10–12 minutes**

Ingredients

- 1 kg / 2 lb 4 oz / 6 ⅔ cups strong plain (all-purpose) white flour
- 2 tsp salt
- 4 tsp fast action dried yeast
- 2 tsp caster (superfine) sugar
- 55 g / 2 oz / ½ cup butter, cubed
- 250 ml / 9 fl. oz / 1 cup semi-skimmed milk
- 450 ml / 16 fl. oz / 1 ½ cups lukewarm water
- a little extra plain (all purpose) white flour for dusting
- 55 g / 1 oz / ⅓ cup white sesame seeds
- 30 g / 1 oz / 2 tbsp black sesame seeds
- 30 g / 1 oz / 2 tbsp black poppy seeds

Method

1. Mix the flour, salt, sugar and yeast in a bowl. Rub in the butter, using your fingertips, until the mixture resembles breadcrumbs.

2. Add the milk and water to the bowl and mix with your hands until you have a rough dough. Knead on a floured surface, with an adult's help, for 12-15 minutes.

3. Let the dough rest in a covered bowl for one hour before kneading again briefly and dividing into 12 balls.

4. Shape each ball into a square and press the seeds into them in combinations of one or two.

5. Arrange them on baking trays and leave in a warm place, covered loosely, for another hour.

6. Preheat the oven to 220°C (200°C fan) / 425F / gas 7; bake the rolls for 10-12 minutes before asking an adult to remove them.

TOP TIP

Replace the seeds with raisins and sultanas to make fruit rolls.

Individual Cauliflower Soufflés

Difficult   Preparation time: 15 minutes   Makes: 4   Cooking time: 12-15 minutes

Ingredients

- 55 g / 2 oz / ½ stick butter, softened
- 30 g / 1 oz / 2 tbsp plain (all purpose) flour
- 250 ml / 9 fl. oz / 1 cup semi-skimmed milk
- 4 large eggs, separated
- 110 g / 4 oz / 1 cup Cheddar, grated
- ½ cauliflower head, prepared into tiny florets
- salt and pepper

TOP TIP

You can switch the cauliflower for the same amount of broccoli for a flash of green colour.

Method

1. Ask an adult to help you preheat the oven to 200°C (180°C fan) / 400F / gas 6 and also brush the inside of four ramekins with half of the butter before chilling.

2. Melt the remaining butter in a saucepan then whisk in the flour until smooth. Cook for 2 minutes then slowly whisk in the milk until it's a thickened sauce.

3. Whisk in the egg yolks, cheese and cauliflower and simmer for 6 minutes before seasoning and setting to one side.

4. Whisk the egg whites in a clean mixing bowl with a pinch of salt until soft peaks form. Whisk a third into the sauce then gently fold in the rest.

5. Divide between the ramekins and bake for 12-15 minutes until golden and puffed.

6. Get an adult to remove them before enjoying!

Cakes

Hedgehog Mikado Cake

Fresh Raspberry Financiers

Individual Mocha Cakes

Chocolate and Raspberry Fondants

Medium   Preparation time: 10–15 minutes   Serves: 6   Cooking time: 11–14 minutes

Ingredients

- 30 g / 1 oz / 2 tbsp butter, melted (for greasing)
- 110 g / 4 oz / ½ cup unsalted butter, cubed
- 110 g / 4 oz / ⅔ cup good-quality dark chocolate, chopped
- 2 medium eggs
- 2 medium egg yolks
- 30 g / 1 oz / 2 tbsp caster (superfine) sugar
- 75 g / 3 oz / ½ cup plain (all purpose) flour
- 150 g / 5 oz / 1 ½ cups raspberries
- 2 tbsp raspberry sauce

Method

1. Ask an adult to preheat the oven to 190°C (170°C fan) / 375F / gas 5 then grease the inside of six small ramekins with melted butter. Chill.

2. Microwave the butter and chocolate together in a microwaveable bowl until just melted. Do this in 30 second bursts; stir in between bursts and get an adult to supervise.

3. Whisk together the whole eggs and two yolks with the sugar in a bowl until pale and thick, then gently fold through the flour and the chocolate mixture.

4. Divide the batter evenly into the ramekins and bake for 11-14 minutes until just set and starting to come away from the sides.

5. Ask an adult to remove them carefully before turning them out onto plates. Garnish with raspberries and sauce.

TOP TIP

If you are feeling adventurous, switch the raspberries for orange segments.

Banana Cheesecake

Easy   Preparation time: 10 minutes   Serves: 6   Cooking time: 10 minutes

Ingredients

- 110 g / 4 oz / ⅔ cup Digestives, crushed
- 70 g / 3 oz / ⅓ cup unsalted butter, melted and cooled
- 30 ml / 1 fl. oz / 2 tbsp lemon juice
- 2 sheets gelatine
- 225 g / 8 oz / 1 cup low-fat cream cheese
- 110 g / 4 oz / ½ cup caster (superfine) sugar
- 225 g / 8 oz / 1 cup Greek yoghurt
- 4 small bananas, peel and mash 3 and slice the remaining one

Method

1. Mix the Digestives and melted butter in a bowl until it looks like wet sand. Pack the mixture into the base and sides of a 1 lb loaf tin with an adult's help.

2. Mix the lemon juice and gelatine in a saucepan and dissolve over a medium heat, stirring occasionally.

3. Beat together the cream cheese and the sugar in a large mixing bowl, and then add the Greek yoghurt and the gelatine mixture, mixing again until smooth.

4. Fold through most of the mashed banana and spoon the mixture into the biscuit base, then spread the rest of the mashed banana on top.

5. Cover the cheesecake with cling film and chill for at least three hours before unwrapping and decorating with banana slices on top.

TOP TIP

If you want to make the cheesecake even yummier, drizzle chocolate sauce on top before eating.

Strawberry Jam Roly Poly

Easy   Preparation time: 10 minutes   Makes: 8   Cooking time: 14–18 minutes

Ingredients

- 110 g / 4 oz / ½ cup caster (superfine) sugar
- 110 g / 4 oz / ½ cup margarine, softened
- 110 g / 4 oz / ⅔ self-raising flour, sifted
- 2 large eggs
- 1 tsp vanilla extract
- 150 g / 5 oz / ⅔ cup seedless strawberry jam
- 30 g / 1 oz / ½ cup icing (confectioners') sugar

Method

1. Ask an adult to help you preheat the oven to 180°C (160°C fan) / 350F / gas 4 and line a 12" x 4" x 3" jelly roll pan with greaseproof paper.

2. Mix the caster sugar, margarine, flour, eggs and vanilla extract in a bowl and stir really well for 3-4 minutes until it's smooth.

3. Scrape the batter into the lined pan and bake for 14-18 minutes until risen and a cake tester comes out clean when inserted.

4. Ask an adult to help you remove it from the oven. Leave it to cool then turn out onto a flat surface and spread the top with jam.

5. Roll into a log shape and arrange on a plate before dusting with icing sugar and eating.

TOP TIP

For a more luxurious version, spread the log with whipped cream before the jam.

Layered Sponge Cream Cake

Medium

Preparation time: 15 minutes

Serves: 12

Cooking time: 15–20 minutes

Ingredients

- 330 g / 11 ½ oz / 1 ½ cups margarine, softened
- 330 g / 11 ½ oz / 1 ½ cups caster (superfine) sugar
- 300 g / 10 ½ oz / 2 cups plain (all purpose) flour, sifted
- 30 g / 1 oz / 2 tbsp cornflour (cornstarch)
- 6 large eggs
- 2 tsp vanilla extract
- 30 g / 1 oz / 2 tbsp cocoa powder
- 55 ml / 2 fl. oz / ¼ cup whole milk
- a few drops of natural orange food dye
- 1 tsp natural green food dye
- 450 ml / 16 fl. oz / 2 cups whipping cream
- 65 g / 2 ½ oz / ½ cup icing (confectioners') sugar

Method

1. Ask an adult to preheat the oven to 180°C (160°C fan) / 350F / gas 4 and line six 7" cake tins with greaseproof paper.

2. Beat together the margarine, sugar, flour, cornflour, eggs and vanilla in a mixing bowl, taking turns with an adult to mix.

3. Once smooth, spoon one-sixth of the batter into another bowl and add the cocoa and milk before beating well.

4. Spoon one-fifth into another bowl and dye orange. Split the remaining batter in two and dye one green

5. Scrape the batters into the tins and bake for 15-20 minutes until a cake tester comes out clean. Whip the cream with the icing sugar until soft and pillowy.

6. Ask an adult to remove the cakes and turn them out when cool. Spread with cream before sandwiching together.

TOP TIP

This cake goes really well with fresh berries in between the layers of cream.

Hedgehog Mikado Cake

 Medium

 Preparation time: 10 minutes

 Makes: 10-12

 Cooking time: 35-45 minutes

Ingredients

- 150 g / 5 oz / ⅔ cup margarine, softened
- 150 g / 5 oz / ⅔ cup caster (superfine) sugar
- 150 g / 5 oz / 1 cup self-raising flour
- 55 ml / 2 fl. oz / ½ cup whole milk
- 50 g / 2 oz / ⅓ cup cocoa
- 3 large eggs

To decorate

- 450 g / 1 lb / 2 cups chocolate spread
- 200 g / 7 oz mixed chocolate fingers
- 50 g / 2 oz / ⅓ cup chocolate sprinkles
- 2 white marshmallows
- 2 liquorice rounds
- 1 round raspberry jelly
- 1 orange jelly bean

Method

1. Ask an adult to preheat the oven to 160°C (140° fan) / 325F / gas 3 and grease and line a 1 lb pudding bowl.

2. Mix all the sponge ingredients in a bowl until smooth before scraping into the pudding bowl and baking for 35-45 minutes until a cake tester comes out clean from the centre.

3. Get an adult to help remove the sponge from the oven and leave it to cool.

4. When it's cool, turn it out onto a flat cake stand; carefully warm the chocolate spread in a microwave and pour over the cake.

5. When the spread starts to set, decorate with the chocolate fingers for spines, marshmallow and liquorice for eyes, raspberry jelly for the nose and a jelly bean for the mouth.

6. Finish by decorating with chocolate sprinkles before eating.

TOP TIP

You could replace some of the fingers with candles to use as a birthday cake.

White Chocolate Muffins

Easy   Preparation time: 10-15 minutes   Makes: 16   Cooking time: 15-20 minutes

Ingredients

- 300 g / 10 ½ oz / 2 cups plain (all purpose) flour
- 175 ml / 8 fl. oz / ½ cup whole milk
- 150 g / 5 oz / ⅔ cup golden caster (superfine) sugar
- 110 ml / 4 fl. oz / ½ cup sunflower oil
- 100 g / 3 ½ oz / ⅔ cup white chocolate, chopped
- 3 tsp baking powder
- 1 large egg
- ½ tsp salt

Method

1. Preheat the oven with an adult's help to 190°C (170°C fan) / 375F / gas 5 and line a large muffin tin with 16 cases.

2. Melt 75 g of the chocolate in a microwave, asking an adult to help supervise, then let it cool for three minutes.

3. Mix the sugar, flour, salt and baking powder in a bowl. Add the egg, oil, melted chocolate and milk then stir briefly until you have a lumpy yet moist batter.

4. Spoon the batter into cases and bake for 15-20 minutes until risen and a cake tester comes out clean.

5. Ask an adult to move the muffin tray to a wire rack to cool.

6. Once cool, shave the remaining chocolate on top of the muffins before eating.

TOP TIP

Shave milk, dark and white chocolate on top instead of just white, to add colour and flavour.

Fresh Raspberry Financiers

Medium   Preparation time: 10 minutes   Makes: 12   Cooking time: 15-18 minutes

Ingredients

- 150 g / 5 oz / 1 ½ cups raspberries
- 110 g / 4 oz / ½ cup caster (superfine) sugar
- 110 g / 4 oz / ½ cup slightly salted butter, softened
- 110 g / 4 oz / 1 cup ground almonds
- 30 g / 1 oz / 2 tbsp plain (all purpose) flour, sifted
- 3 medium egg whites
- 1 tbsp icing (confectioners') sugar
- 1 tbsp unsalted butter, softened
- a pinch of salt

Method

1. Ask an adult to help you preheat the oven to 180°C (160°C fan) / 350F / gas 4 and grease a 12-hole financier tin with unsalted butter; chill.

2. With adult supervision, melt the butter in a saucepan until it starts to turn brown and smell nutty before straining it through a sieve and into a bowl.

3. Mix the flour, salt, almonds and caster sugar in a bowl and whisk in the egg whites before folding through the melted butter; chill for 30 minutes.

4. Spoon the batter into the tin and dot each cake hole with some raspberries; bake for 15-18 minutes until golden and risen.

5. Ask an adult to remove the tin to a wire rack to cool.

6. Turn out the financiers and dust with icing sugar before enjoying.

TOP TIP

You could swap the raspberries for seedless black grapes or pistachios.

Chocolate and Smartie Fondants

Medium   Preparation time: 10–15 minutes   Makes: 6   Cooking time: 11–14 minutes

Ingredients

- 110 g / 4 oz / ⅔ cup good-quality dark chocolate, chopped
- 110 g / 4 oz / ½ cup unsalted butter, cubed
- 75 g / 3 oz / ½ cup Smarties
- 75 g / 3 oz / ½ cup plain (all purpose) flour
- 30 g / 1 oz / 2 tbsp butter, melted
- 30 g / 1 oz / 2 tbsp caster (superfine) sugar
- 2 medium eggs
- 2 medium egg yolks

TOP TIP

You can use chocolate covered raisins instead of Smarties for a twist.

Method

1. Ask an adult to preheat the oven to 190°C (170°C fan) / 375F / gas 5 and grease the inside of six small ramekins with melted butter; chill.

2. Microwave the butter and chocolate together in a microwaveable bowl, until just melted. Do this in 30 second bursts, stirring in between bursts.

3. Whisk together the whole eggs, egg yolks and sugar in a bowl until pale and thick, then gently fold through the flour, chocolate mixture and most of the Smarties.

4. Divide the batter evenly into the ramekins and bake for 11-14 minutes until just set and starting to come away from the sides.

5. Ask an adult to remove them carefully before turning them out onto plates; garnish with Smarties on top.

Cherry Almond Brioche Cake

Easy   Preparation time: 10–15 minutes   Makes: 12   Cooking time: 15 minutes

Ingredients

- 2 x medium brioche loaves
- 400 g / 14 oz / 2 cups canned cherries, drained, with some juice reserved
- 100 g / 3 ½ oz / ½ cup unsalted butter, softened
- 40 g / 1 ½ oz / ⅓ cup flaked (slivered) almonds
- 1 tbsp icing (confectioners') sugar
- a small handful of cherries, to garnish

Method

1. Ask an adult to help you preheat the oven to 180°C (160°C fan) / 350F / gas 4 and to line a 7" round, springform cake tin.

2. With an adult supervising, cut the brioche loaves into slices and butter them. Use half to line the base of the tin, cutting them to shape to fit snugly.

3. Spoon the cherries and their juice on top and place the other brioche slices on top, cutting them to size to fit.

4. Bake for 15 minutes to warm through before asking an adult to remove the cake from the oven.

5. Let it cool before turning out and garnishing with flaked almonds, a dusting of icing sugar and pop the cherries on top.

TOP TIP

A mixture of raspberries and cranberry jelly in the middle is equally tasty.

Chocolate and Almond Cake

Medium   Preparation time: 15 minutes   Serves: 8   Cooking time: 45–55 minutes

Ingredients

- 225 g / 8 oz / 1 ½ cup dark chocolate, chopped
- 110 g / 4 oz / ½ cup caster (superfine) sugar
- 100 g / 3 ½ oz / ½ cup unsalted butter, diced
- 75 g / 3 oz / ½ cup ground almonds
- 4 large eggs, separated
- a pinch of salt

To decorate

- 50 g / 2 oz / ⅓ cup dark chocolate squares
- 50 g / 2 oz / ½ cup flaked (slivered) almonds
- 30 g / 1 oz / ½ cup icing (confectioners') sugar

Method

1. Ask an adult to preheat the oven to 150°C (130°C fan) / 300F / gas 2 and to grease and line an 8" springform cake tin.

2. Place the chocolate and butter in a heatproof bowl and microwave in 30-second bursts, stirring in between, until melted. Beat in the egg yolks and caster sugar.

3. Whisk the egg whites in another bowl with a pinch of salt until thick and glossy, then fold into the chocolate mixture.

4. Fold through the ground almonds and pour into the tin, then bake for 45-55 minutes until the cake starts to come away from the sides of the tin.

5. Ask an adult to remove it to a wire rack to cool before carefully turning out and decorating with flaked almonds, chocolate squares and a dusting of icing sugar on top.

TOP TIP

Instead of using chocolate squares on top, why not grate white chocolate over the cake?

Pine Nut Sponge Fingers

Easy   Preparation time: 10–15 minutes   Makes: 18   Cooking time: 18–20 minutes

Ingredients

- 110 g / 4 oz / ⅔ cup self-raising flour, sifted
- 110 g / 4 oz / ½ cup golden caster (superfine) sugar
- 110 g / 4 oz / ½ cup margarine, softened
- 100 g / 3 oz / ½ cup seedless raspberry jam, warmed
- 50 g / 2 oz / ½ pine nuts
- 36 raspberries
- 2 large eggs
- 1 tsp vanilla extract

Method

1. Ask an adult to preheat the oven to 180°C (160°C fan) / 350F / gas 4 and line a 6" cake tin with greaseproof paper.

2. Beat the flour, sugar, margarine, eggs and vanilla extract in a bowl until really smooth before spooning into the tin.

3. Bake the sponge for 18-20 minutes until a cake tester comes out clean from its centre; ask an adult to remove it to a wire rack to cool.

4. Turn it out once cool and spread the top with warmed jam before cutting into 18 small fingers.

5. Top with a couple of raspberries and a few pine nuts before eating.

TOP TIP

You could use hazelnuts, pistachios or almonds instead of pine nuts on top of the fingers.

Marble Cake

Medium   Preparation time: 10 minutes   Makes: 8–10   Cooking time: 45–55 minutes

Ingredients

- 225 g / 8 oz / 1 cup unsalted butter, softened
- 225 g / 8 oz / 1 cup caster (superfine) sugar
- 225 g / 8 oz / 1 ½ cups self-raising flour
- 30 g / 1 oz / 2 tbsp good-quality cocoa powder
- 4 large eggs
- 3 tbsp whole milk
- 2 tsp vanilla extract

Method

1. Ask an adult to help you preheat the oven to 180°C (160°C fan) / 350F / gas 4 and line a 2 lb loaf tin with greaseproof paper.

2. Mix together all the ingredients apart from the cocoa powder and milk in a bowl, beating until smooth.

3. Divide the batter into two bowls and add the cocoa powder and milk to one of them, beating well.

4. Spoon half the vanilla batter into the tin, top with two-thirds of the chocolate, then top with the rest of the vanilla and then the rest of the chocolate.

5. Tap the tin to release any air and bake for 45-55 minutes until a cake tester comes out clean from the centre.

6. Get an adult to move it to a wire rack to cool before turning out, slicing and serving.

TOP TIP

This cake goes really well with a dollop of whipped cream or Greek yoghurt on the side.

Individual Vanilla Sponge Cakes

Easy   Preparation time: 10-15 minutes   Makes: 6   Cooking time: 18-22 minutes

Ingredients

- 110 g / 4 oz / ⅔ cup self-raising flour, sifted
- 110 g / 4 oz / ½ cup caster (superfine) sugar
- 110 g / 4 oz / ½ cup unsalted butter, softened
- 2 large eggs
- 2 tsp vanilla extract
- a pinch of salt

Method

1. Ask an adult to help you preheat the oven to 180°C (160°C fan) / 350F / gas 4 and line six individual loaf tins with greaseproof paper.

2. Mix together all the ingredients in a bowl until really smooth.

3. Fill the tins evenly with the batter and bake them on a tray for 18-22 minutes until a cake tester comes out clean from their centres.

4. Ask an adult to remove them to a wire rack to cool before turning them out onto greaseproof paper and serving.

TOP TIP

Swirl some caramel sauce through the batter before spooning into the tins and baking.

Individual Mocha Cakes

Medium   Preparation time: 15 minutes   Makes: 4   Cooking time: 15-18 minutes

Ingredients

- 110 g / 4 oz / ⅔ cup self-raising flour, sifted
- 110 g / 4 oz / ½ cup caster (superfine) sugar
- 110 g / 4 oz / ½ cup margarine, softened
- 2 large eggs
- 1 tsp vanilla extract

To decorate

- 200 g / 7 oz / 1 cup ready-made chocolate buttercream
- 150 g / 5 oz / 1 cup dark chocolate, grated
- 4 raspberries
- 2 tbsp boiling water
- 2 tsp instant espresso powder
- 1 tbsp cocoa powder

Method

1. Ask an adult to help preheat the oven to 180°C (160°C fan) / 350F / gas 4 and line four individual cake moulds.

2. Beat together all the sponge ingredients in a bowl until smooth. Divide between the moulds and bake for 15-18 minutes until a cake tester comes out clean from their centres.

3. Ask an adult to remove them to a wire rack to cool.

4. Dissolve the espresso powder in the boiling water and add it to the buttercream in a bowl. Beat well until smooth and spread a little on the outside of the cakes. Roll the iced outsides in the grated chocolate.

5. Spoon the remaining icing into a piping bag and pipe it on top of the cakes in a swirl.

6. Garnish with a raspberry and dusting of cocoa powder before enjoying.

TOP TIP

Instead of using grated dark chocolate, use white chocolate for an interesting contrast.

Index